Being Patient With Yourself

Being Patient With Yourself

StoryTerrace

Text Aissa Martell, on behalf of StoryTerrace

First print January 2023

StoryTerrace

www.StoryTerrace.com

This book is dedicated in memory of my father, mother, and brother. Walter Mitchell Jackson, Inez Jackson, Victor Darnell Jackson respectively. In addition, I would like to thank family and friends who have been an inspiration in my life during times of adversity. Thank you for your social support. I love you.

CONTENTS

1

LIFE IN ALAMEDA

Love is patient; love is kind. It does not envy;
it does not boast. It is not proud; it is not rude.
It is not self-seeking; it is not easily angered. It
keeps no record of wrong. Love does not delight
in evil but rejoices with truth. It always protects,
always trusts, always hopes, always preserves.
Love never fails.
Corinthians 13:4–8

My father was originally from Ferriday, Louisiana, and my mother was from Chickasha, Oklahoma. These two Southern teens moved to Alameda, California, and met at Alameda High. That's when Walter Mitchell Jackson and Inez Sanders fell in love. My parents got married on March 28th, 1952, in Oakland California, and moved in with my paternal grandparents. I come from a faith-based family that was extremely business savvy. My grandfather owned Pitts Construction and a large Victorian three-story home on Jay Street, where my siblings and I lived the first years of our lives.

My brother Victor Darnell Jackson was born three years before me, and my older sister Donna Rochelle Jackson is only 15 months older than me. We grew up close and had loving parents and grandparents that we equally adored. We had wonderful times together. My parents would take us to Washington Park in Alameda, and Alameda Beach, the latter of which left a lasting impression on me. I used to play in the ocean with my brother and sister until one day, my brother mischievously led me to an area with seaweed on the ocean floor. He laughed hysterically when I stepped in it, but I was shell-shocked and peed myself, and I haven't been in the water since.

Since my sister and I were so close in age, we played together a lot. We would play with our Chatty Cathy and Barbie dolls together. Once, when I cut all of my Barbie doll's hair off, I was disappointed with the results and wanted to play with my sister's doll, so I took it from her. My sister didn't see any reason to pay for the mistake that I had made and demanded I return her doll. I wasn't happy with that so I broke off her Barbie doll's head. Luckily, it was able to be snapped back on.

Moments like these with my siblings would be exchanged like glimmering tokens amongst us in years to come. Memories are a way to hold onto the ones we love, in a spirit of days gone by. Far away from our days in the ocean, we could look back and embrace the past and laugh, even in the most trying of times.

My father kept us entertained with games of peekaboo under the kitchen table, and after my older siblings had to go to bed for the night, my father would hold me in his lap and rock me to sleep. We attended services every Sunday at the Church of the Living God in Oakland. My mother and father were always very well groomed, stylish, and well put together, and they made sure their children were as well. My mom would dress my sister and me for church in similar outfits: Mary Jane shoes, Mary Jane ruffle socks, and dainty purses. We wore beautiful dresses with petticoats, and we had ribbons in our hair. One day after my mother got me dressed up for church, I snuck outside and made mud pies. This act of insurrection made my mother cry. She had to put together another outfit for me to wear to church, and that would surely make us late. My parents instilled religion in me, and God has been a guiding light for all of my life. Although, with life's ups and downs and twists and turns, I cannot say I always heeded the call or was as loyal in my faith as I should have been.

My parents provided me with a strong foundation, mentally, emotionally, and spiritually. They instilled in me everything I needed to grow and become a success. They taught me what love is and how to love and accept love. Later on in my life with trials and tribulations, it was all too easy to lose sight of what my parents had instilled in me. It took a lot of patience with myself and self-compassion to find my way back to this place of love and self-acceptance on my own.

The neighborhood we lived in at my grandparents' house was all Caucasian. When I went to kindergarten, I was the only black student in my class. One day, when my mom had to stay in bed because she was very ill, my grandmother dropped me off at school. I can't remember my kindergarten teacher's name, but on this day, she delivered an experience I'll never forget. She was a Caucasian woman, and after the other students and I turned in our assignments, she selected mine from the pile, put it on the board, and told all of the kids in my class that I was dumb and stupid. I was only five years old, and the year was 1962. I didn't know what racism was. I had not been told that I would be treated differently than the Caucasian students in my class because of my race. But I knew in my gut that something was very wrong. I looked at my teacher, and I said, "I'm never coming back to this class again," and I stood up and walked out of class.

I was very embarrassed, and I didn't know why it had happened. I also didn't really know how to get home, but I followed my gut, decided to take my chances, and started walking home. When I got to the crosswalk, the crossing guard stopped me and asked why I was leaving school and asked me where I was going, and I said "I'm going home." the crossing guard asked me again, "Why are you leaving school?"

"I just want to leave school," I replied. I was afraid to tell her what had happened to me. I was afraid, embarrassed, and ashamed. The crossing guard let me be on my way and, without really knowing how to get there, I walked all the way home. I was just a little bitty thing, but I was able to persevere and make it home on my own. When I got there, I walked up the steps and knocked on the door, and my grandmother answered. She was shocked and said, "Oh, my God! What are you doing home?" I was afraid to tell my grandmother because I thought I was going to get a spanking. And to this day, I don't recall ever telling my mom because she was very sick.

My grandmother took me back to school. I walked into class, and the teacher was in tears. She didn't know what had happened to me. I had just disappeared. So when I got back to the class, her perspective, and her attitude, had changed. She didn't tell my grandmother what she had done, and I kept the secret tucked inside myself.

Racism at the time of my birth was unknown to me. My parents kept us far away from this terrible emotional rhetoric. They encouraged us to think about shared morals and values, encouraging aspirations with positive thinking. It wasn't until I was an adult that I noticed the racism that surrounded me and my parents at my birth. On my birth certificate, Alameda Hospital labeled my father as a negro, and my beautiful mother as a negress. I was extremely offended upon making this discovery. However, due to my experience as a five-year-old at Woodstock Elementary School, I was not surprised. In Alameda, black people were constantly being pulled over by the cops and harassed, and it was not always wise for black people to stay out after certain hours in the evening. My siblings and I didn't experience a lot of racism due to living there because our parents did their best to shelter us from this type of adversity. Growing up we didn't see color, we didn't see white or black, we saw people as people. Because my parents were faith-based they taught us to just love one another.

When my siblings and I were growing up on Jay Street there were a few Caucasian kids we would play with, but there was one lady that lived around the corner from us, in a green house, that I recall sicking her dogs on me. I was skating in the neighborhood and she opened the door and said, "Get!" Her dogs started chasing me and, frightened, I started skating very fast home. When I got there I ran up the stairs of my grandparent's house in tears. I still had my skates on and I'm not even sure how I got up the steps. My grandmother tried to console me by saying the dogs just wanted to play, but I didn't get that impression. As a child, there are some things that you just don't forget.

There's racism all over the world and we must learn how to love one another and not stereotype each other. Black, white, light-skinned, or dark-skinned, we're all equal and worthy of love and respect. In this day and age, black people are still under attack, we must try to learn how to get along, love and respect each other, "God so loved the world that he gave his only begotten son, that who so ever believes in him shall not perish but have everlasting life." Through God's sacrificial love, we must learn to love each other. God so loved the world, not just one race. We all must show integrity, love, and respect for one another.

I feel very bad for my parents and what they must have endured. Reading my birth certificate I was heartbroken for them. I can't imagine the kind of racism they witnessed. My aunt told me that my mother had a hard time fitting in because she was light-skinned. I didn't see it firsthand and I only knew of racism in the 60s from watching TV. During the black panther movement, my brother wanted a black panther jacket, but my father told him "no way." They sheltered us from stereotypes and any obstacles that would prevent us from viewing people as the same. They had been through racism themselves and they did not want us to go through it. I will always respect the fact that our parents tried to protect us from any and all racism. They never spoke badly about anybody no matter what they went through as children growing up in the south.

Because my family had their own business, and we were well off financially, I feel we were accepted more than other black families. Alameda's demographic was primarily doctors, lawyers, and attorneys. If you didn't have money as a black person you didn't live in Alameda. Shortly after my teacher embarrassed me in class, our family moved out of Alameda.

The best love story is the one you share together

Mr. and Mrs. Alex Massey

request the honour of your presence

at the marriage of their daughter

Inez Sanders

to

Mr. Walter M. Jackson

on Saturday, the twenty-eighth of March

at seven o'clock in the evening

Eight nineteen Thirty-seventh Street

Oakland, California

Reception

immediately following the ceremony

Eight seventy-one Fifty-third Street

Oakland, California

Memories Full of Love

God's Precious Singing Angels

Linda's Mom, Inez, and Little Aunt Lavonia posing for picture day

2

SKATES AND PLAY DATES

Our Father which art in heaven. Hallowed be thy name.
Thy kingdom come. Thy will be done, on earth as it is
in heaven. Give us this day thy daily bread. Forgive us our
debts, as we forgive our debtors. And lead us not into
temptation. But deliver us from evil. For thine is the
kingdom, the power, and glory forever and ever. Amen.
Matthew 6:9–13

My parents purchased their first home on Arthur Street in
Oakland California when I was around seven years old. This
would be the arena of many laughs, get-togethers, and life lessons
for decades to come. My siblings and I attended Markham
Elementary School. I vividly remember one of my teachers from
Markham Elementary, Miss Pemberton. She was an African
American teacher, and she was very strict. She kept a bunch of
rulers tied up with a rubber band for whenever there was an
infraction to her rules. If anyone made a noise in her class, those

rulers came down on the desk like a bolt of lightning, and she would tell everyone to hush.

My parents ran a very structured and clean household. My mom made sure our clothes were ironed, and our shoes were polished the night before we went to school. We were not allowed to iron our clothes in the morning. We never went to school in wrinkled clothes, and we showed up every day in sparkling white Buck Oxford shoes. My siblings and I were good students and always behaved, so much so my sister and I were two of several students who were chosen to attend an opera. I don't recall the name of the opera, but I do recall my sister and me wearing beautiful blue and white dresses, with a jacket and of course our Mary Jane shoes with ruffled socks. We learned at a young age that the age-old adage of "dress for success" is exactly true.

My mother worked at Liberty House in Oakland. Liberty House was a five-story department store, so she was always current on the latest fashion and trends. My parents were always fashionable and well put together. The sense of pride they had in their appearance was instilled in us as children, and it did not go unnoticed.

I was still attending Markham Elementary School when I began child modeling. It all started when I was selected to participate in a Christmas pageant at the Oakland Coliseum. I was dressed as Raggedy Ann for the pageant, and I thoroughly enjoyed myself. The confidence it takes to walk down a runway exuded from me naturally, and the work began to snowball. I began working as a child model for various retailers at Liberty

House, like Montgomery Ward, and Fairy Land was my favorite. I was never signed with an agency; however, I would enjoy numerous freelance modeling gigs well into adulthood.

Although our neighborhood in Oakland had more people of color than the neighborhood we lived in with my grandparents in Alameda, we were only one of five black families on the block when we first moved in. It was mostly Caucasian, and our Caucasian neighbors were not very kind, but they accepted us. However, when we moved on the block, they started to move out. And over the years as black people started to move in, the Caucasian people started to move out.

No matter of the demographic of our neighborhood, we enjoyed ourselves immensely, and our home was a place of much joy and laughter. By the time I reached junior high, our home was host to the neighborhood kids and many friends and family. We had a red front porch with a black fence, and my dad would watch over us from the porch as we would skate and ride bikes with the kids from the neighborhood. My sweet father would prepare French fries for everybody. He fried up a big old bag of crispy French fries and everybody would just dig in, and it was delicious!

When we were not playing with dolls in the front yard or skating and biking throughout the neighborhood, we enjoyed a large backyard that had an apple tree, a peach tree, a pear tree, and a plum tree. Everybody from the neighborhood would come to eat fruit, as well as play tether ball, badminton, checkers, and hula-hoop. My parents bought many games for us to enjoy like Sorry, Monopoly, Mousetrap, and Twister, and once even an

Ouija board, which frightened us so much my parents threw it in the garbage. And of course hide and go seek. We played under the watchful eyes of our parents; their love was tangible, and we had wonderful times.

I attended Frick Junior High School, where I ran track and was an honor roll student. I held on to some of my honor roll certificates from junior high for a long time. And true to form, my mother kept us up to date and in the latest fashions. At this time, it was sizzlers with bloomers underneath, straight from Liberty House. On Saturdays, my dad took me, my sister, and our neighbor across the street, Juana Porter, to the skating rink in San Leandro. We kept up our Saturday skate night tradition faithfully until a few years into high school.

Another one of my and my sister's best friends was Anita Martin. Our parents were friends with her parents, Maxine and Gene Martin. My parents would go over to their house for get-togethers, and left to our own devices, we would go to her room and play. One time when I was in the sixth grade, we snuck a beer out of the refrigerator. We passed it around, and each scoffed at its taste, and we did that for several rounds until we finally threw it down the toilet. We never touched another beer.

We loved going over to Gene and Maxine Martin's house, skating, and we just enjoyed that life. It was free. I remember watching my parents slow-dance to old-school classic songs that they loved and gazing into each other's eyes with so much love like they were caught on a breeze. Just watching them love each other was magnificent and beautiful. When you grow up and you watch your parents set an example, you mimic them and try to live the way they do.. Looking back, I feel I may have tried to have the relationship that my parents had to the extent that I lost sight of myself.

My parents spoiled us every Christmas. Whatever we wanted we got. We always had a beautiful Christmas tree, and we were delighted to find bikes, roller skates, and clothes by the tree on Christmas morning. One Christmas, I got a beautiful pair of skates, and I spent the day outside rolling along on my new set of wheels. I was having so much fun that when my mother called us in for dinner, the last thing I wanted to do was sit still. But I obeyed my mother and sat down at the table. However, I could not truly be still; I was too antsy and kept leaning back in my chair. My parents repeatedly told me to stop, but I kept dreaming of my skates and was still euphoric about the day, and I kept playing by leaning back in my chair until my butt hit the ground. My brother and sister laughed uproariously, and my parents scolded me. I sat back in my chair and managed to sit still, but I still had a few tricks up my sleeve.

After we had finished dinner, the dishes were washed, and my parents were in their room, I got my new skates and coat on and snuck outside. It must have been about nine o'clock, and I was having a wonderful time until my father snatched me up, took me inside the house, and tore my rump up.

My parents loved us very much, but they did not spare the rod. Growing up as children, we used to get our hair pressed all the time so that it would be straight. My mother used a hot comb to straighten our hair. I remember one time while she was pressing my sister's hair, I was relaxing in the family room waiting to get my hair pressed next. My father had just gone grocery shopping, and maybe I was anxious, maybe I was bored, but I decided to open the cinnamon rolls, and I couldn't have just one; I ate the whole pack. At first, I blamed it on my brother, and he got a spanking for nothing. When I told the truth, I tried to ball up under my mom's chair in the kitchen where she was pressing my sister's hair to prevent bearing my punishment. But my father grabbed my leg and got me out from under the chair, and I received the same punishment my brother had endured, except deservedly. My parents made sure to explain to us why we were getting a spanking, so we understood what we did wrong. I know not everybody spanks their kids, but back then, we got a spanking.

We were very family-oriented, and we always had wonderful Christmases and holidays together, with aunts, uncles, cousins, and the whole family. Every Sunday, we attended the Church of the Living God, and I have fond memories of Sunday school and training union and attending services with my family. My family would open up with the Lord's Prayer, and my mom, and her sisters, my aunt Lavonia and aunt Awilder, would sing praises to the Lord. I used to watch in wonder as they would catch the spirit. My parents gave us money to make a contribution to the church. My sister and I put our money in the church, but my brother used to save his 50 cents and buy a delicious piece of chicken breast from Sister Edwards, the church cook. He ate it in the car on the way home from church as my sister and I looked on enviously. My sister and I ate stale cheese puffs, and when we asked our brother for a bite of his chicken, he shook his head. My mother would tell Victor to let us have a bite, and we laughed and giggled and ate stale cheese puffs and a bite of Victor's chicken.

Our family has a heritage of sharing, and I still believe in sharing. I have shared so much in my life that at times it has been to my own detriment. I helped others along their path and neglected to follow my own.

Little Linda Smiley Faces

Donna Sweet As Pie

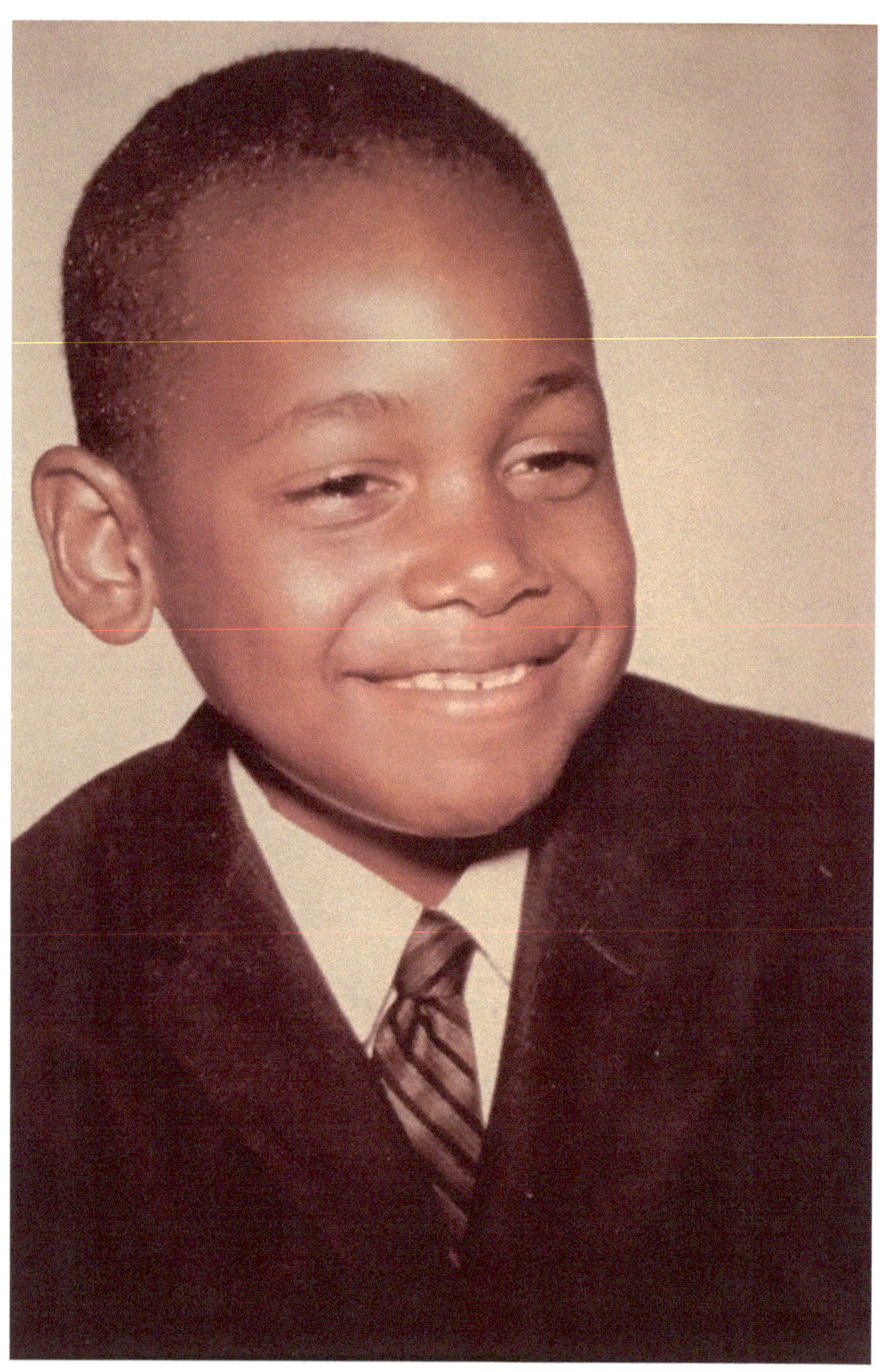

Victor, My Special Brother

A beautiful snapshot with Grandma Leola.

Donna and Linda at Church Of Living God. Bishop James A. McFall Children's Choir.

3

A MOVER AND A SHAKER

Wives, submit to your husbands as to the Lord.
Husbands, love your wives just as Christ loved
the church and gave himself up for her.
Ephesians 5:22 & 25

My life changed in high school, from one end of the spectrum to the other and all the colors in between. I attended Fremont High, and it was beautiful. I was a cheerleader, I wrote for the school newspaper called *The Green and Gold*, and I got my first job at the age of 16 with the California State Unemployment Office, and I worked at the California State Disability Office. I was very vibrant and ambitious. A mover, a shaker, and a motivator. I was always on the go and always had something to do. My mom was very proud of me. I was responsible, I got good grades in school, and had by all accounts a good job at a young age. I would take my checks and offer my parents a portion of them if they wanted them, but they certainly never asked me for anything. It felt good to be able to help my family financially, even if it wasn't needed.

I used to go shopping all the time. It was nice to have my own money. High school is also where I met my daughter's father.

I guess you would say he was my high school sweetheart, although it didn't turn out as it should have. I hadn't been with anyone that intimately before I was with Robert, and I believe he took advantage of my naivety. My parents didn't share the birds and the bees with me, so I think it gave him some pleasure to groom me, a young, naïve girl. To be honest, I really didn't like him because he smothered me, and he wasn't a very nice person. He would make comments calling me stupid and naïve, and my mother definitely did not like him. However, I was naïve; when I got pregnant, I didn't even know I was pregnant. Since my parents never educated me about sex, I didn't know the signs to look out for. I just thought I was sick.

My mother took me to our family doctor in Alameda, and when he relayed the news, my mother was shocked and devastated. She slapped me across my face. She didn't mean to; it was done out of shock. She was in tears; she had so many hopes and dreams for me. She wanted me to go to college, and it just broke her heart. I went through the nine months without her father because once he found out I was pregnant, he didn't want anything to do with me. I mean, literally nothing. I had the support of my family, but at the same time, I was lonely and confused. I was raised in a loving family, and for my daughter's father to just vanish was confounding. But, I kept myself busy and accepted new opportunities when they arose.

Though I was single and pregnant, that didn't stop me from being a mover and a shaker. I graduated from high school early, in January, because I had all the credits that I needed, and I went back in June to accept my diploma and walk across the stage. After I graduated high school, I got my first job in the medical profession at the children's hospital in Oakland. My supervisor was Stella Daniels, and she was my inspiration. We are still friends to this day. I stayed there for 10 years. I still work in the medical profession and have a long resume. After I left the children's hospital, I went to Providence Hospital. I started independent contracting as a medical consultant and traveled to various hospitals in the Bay area. And from an independent contractor, I started working at the Eye Surgery Center of San Francisco as a business office supervisor, and that's where I will retire.

I had my beautiful daughter Demetra in 1976. She was a joy, but it wasn't until after she was born that the word "marriage" came up. My parents were old school and truly saved, and they didn't believe in having a child out of wedlock, and back then, it was frowned upon. So, I was forced to marry Robert, and I felt the marriage was a cover-up. Initially, when we were getting married, he walked away from the altar. Because we were both so young, neither one of us knew any better. However, we both ended up going through with it. During the course of our marriage, there was infidelity, and because of his infidelity, he brought a few diseases home with him. He showed contempt for his child, and he downright hated my mother. He used to come to the house with monkey bites on his neck and would say, "Don't nobody want you. You have a daughter. Don't no man want you with no baby. Don't no man want you with no child. Who are you trying to talk to?" He showed blatant disrespect and was outright rude and mean. It was a lot to put up with in a short amount of time because after six months, we got an annulment, and I moved back in with my parents. Robert never came around to visit his daughter.

Now, I would never accept what I accepted back then as a young mother; it's something I just would not tolerate. But when I was young, I was gullible. I didn't know if I was coming or going, and I was overwhelmed. I learned by my marriage to Robert not to be with a man, even the father of your child if you are not compatible. Everybody wants love and companionship, but sometimes, we try to please our companions so much that we lose sight of ourselves. By losing sight of ourselves, we accept less than we deserve.

My Fremont High Senior Class Photo.

Me back in the day, Fremont High School. Class of 1975 cheerleaders. Win or lose, we loved our team.

Gail, Donna, and I, hanging out back when.

My daughter, Demetra loving Christmas.

My son, Marc — not sure if he wanted to smile or not.

4

BAD THINGS HAPPEN IN THREES

No weapon that is formed against me shall prosper;
and every tongue that shall rise up against thee in
judgment thou shall condemn.
Isaiah 54:17

I had my daughter Demetra when I was 19, and two years later, my mother passed away at the age of 45 on December 19th, 1979. I was devastated. Although I had a baby, I was still a baby myself. When I told Demetra's father that my mother passed away, his response was, "things happen to people who talk too much." And he made fun of my mother. I may forgive him for what he did, but I will never forget, and any trace of respect I had for him was erased at that moment. My mother was truly saved and a child of God and did not deserve to be disrespected on her grave.

Two months after my mother passed away, my brother Victor accidentally killed his son. Victor had moved out of our family home and was living in Oakland with his wife Sheila and their three children, Little Victor Jr, Inez, and Jovonne. At the time, Sheila was a lady of the night, and they both were abusing drugs, so that had some influence over the incident because when it happened, Victor was grieving our mother, and I believe he was on heroin.

Little Victor went into the living room where my brother was lying on the couch. He was just two years old, and he wanted to get dressed so he could go outside and play with the kids in the neighborhood. Victor yelled to Sheila to get his clothes on so he could go outside. When Sheila did not dress him, Little Victor returned to the living room crying because he wanted to go out and play. My brother got frustrated and slapped him. When he did that, Little Victor fell back, and his head hit the edge of the coffee table, and he never woke up. My brother picked him up, and he was limp. He took him to the bedroom, lay him down on the bed, called the police, and had himself arrested. He was arrested in February 1980. I think it was just too much for him.

We were all devastated, my sister, my father, and I. It would have been horrible at any time, but so close to the loss of my mother, it carried extra weight. My father was beside himself. When Victor first went to prison, he was sent to San Quentin. I didn't visit him when he was in San Quentin because I was just too overwhelmed, but my father and my sister did. My brother went from San Quentin to Vacaville Prison, to Folsom Prison and back to Vacaville Prison in his lifetime.

It really broke my father. He went to see Victor all the time and took care of him financially with everything he needed. He had lost his wife and then his son to prison, but he stayed strong to support my brother as much as he could. They say bad things happen in threes, and the loss of my mother, my nephew Little Victor, and my brother to the prison system was profoundly life-changing for us all.

I can't say I made the best choices while I was going through this time in my life, especially when it came to men. But the silver lining is that I had my beautiful son Marc in 1983. His father and I did not stay together. Unfortunately, we did not have a strong foundation because I chose to be with him out of spite due to the adversity that I went through in my previous marriage. It was a poor decision on my part. But Marc was truly a blessing. Since Marc's father and I split, he has never been a part of his life, and never communicated with him, and I knew from previous experiences not to go down that road again. However, I persevered through it all and welcomed a beautiful bundle of joy.

My precious mother, Inez Jackson. Gone to soon at the age 45. You are forever in our hearts.

My precious father, Walter Mitchell Jackson. Gone to soon at age 56. We will never forget you.

Memories are timeless treasures. We love you! The both of you are greatly missed.

My special brother, Victor suffered much loss.

5

WORK AND PLAY

Love the Lord thy God with all your heart and with
all your soul and with all your mind. This is the first
and greatest commandment. Love your neighbor as yourself.
Matthew 22:37–39

Although I was a single mother, old habits die hard, and I
was still a mover and a shaker. I worked full-time at the children's
hospital and modeled on the weekends. I still made time for
my lifetime love of skating, attended church, and I made the
time to go out dancing and having fun. The clubs that I liked to
go out to back then were Ivy's, Jack London, Wine and Roses,
and Silks in Emeryville. I also went to the Circle Star to see
various performances. I remember seeing Teddy Pendergrass
there. The performances there were unique because they had a
revolving stage.

They tore the Circle Star down in 1993 because it brought too
many black people to San Carlos. There were a lot of black artists
that performed at the Circle Star, and we would go out in droves

to the performances. Everybody adored going to the Circle Star because you could see anybody and everybody, and there wasn't a bad seat because the stage revolved a full 360 degrees. But they wanted all of the black people out of there, so they tore it down.

I did a lot of freelance modeling gigs on the weekends. I modeled for various organizations, like the NAACP. I modeled for Jerry Ivory, Elle Tyner, Bambi, ETM Models, and The Gingerbread House in Oakland. I did numerous shows as a freelance model, and I would get a babysitter for my kids. My sister Donna used to watch my kids for me, and my mentor from work, Stella Daniels, used to help me out as well.

Even though I had a full-time job, I had full benefits, I was self-sufficient, and I made sure my children were taken care of and had clothes on their backs and shoes on their feet, I still wanted to go because I was so young. I felt like I was missing out. Even though I was a good mother, I still could have been a better one. In hindsight, I should have spent more time at home instead of jumping into the action.

And even though I was going to church, I wasn't grounded like I should have been. And was I saved? Yes, I was saved, but I feel I was disloyal. There was no loyalty there; there was no loyalty to God, and there was no loyalty to myself.

A family that prays together stays together.

6
WORK AND PLAY

God said that in this matter no one should wrong his
brother or sister or take advantage of him. The Lord will
punish men and women for such sins as we have already
told you and warned you.
Thessalonians 4:6

On November 22, 1986, my father passed away. He was
heartbroken after my mother passed away, and then losing
his grandson and his son going to prison within a few months
afterward was just too much for him. He died of a broken heart.
My sister Donna had gotten married and moved out of our
family home before then. But my two young children and I were
still in my family home. My daughter was 10, and my son was
three at the time. It was very hard for me to lose the foundation
that had always supported me and been there for me, mentally,
emotionally, and spiritually, too.

After my father passed away, my sister and I took over looking
after our brother in prison. When he was in Vacaville, my sister

didn't visit him as much because I lived closer, but when he was in Folsom, she was the closest to him. I visited him quite a lot in Vacaville. His children didn't take the initiative to visit him, so it was mostly my sister and me, but I was the one who primarily took care of him financially because my sister did not work for long after she got married. I was down for him, therefore, I took care of it. I made a decent salary. I can't say I made a lot of money, but my dad was no longer there, I had to take over. Financially, it was hard for me at times, but I paid for years and years and years for the commissary. I did it all: Clothes, food, TVs, radios, CDs, DVDs. I had to supply everything he needed, with little to no help from anyone else.

When I was at home, I was very lonely, and there was a friend of the family who was significantly older than me, and he happened to be a millionaire who decided to check up on me. He had other motives, but shortly after my father passed away, he started coming to the house and leaving groceries on the front porch. He was an older gentleman, and in addition to the groceries, he was overly kind.

I remember it vividly. I was still in my parents' house because it was right after my father died, and he came to the house wearing this green muumuu, and he said, "You're really down and out with both your parents gone. Why don't you let me take you shopping?" And I said, "OK," and he took me shopping. He took me to Bloomingdales, and that was the first time I had ever seen a $200 pair of shoes. I know it's not much now, but back in the '80s, it was expensive.

One time, he bought me lavish, beautiful attire because I was going to a convention out of town in Oklahoma, and he bought me all these beautiful clothes that were outrageously expensive. Before he handed them over to me, he took the clothes with him and said, "When you get a chance one day after work, I want you to come by my office and you can pick up the clothes." And I said, "OK, no problem." I didn't think anything of it. However, when I got to his office, he wanted sex. Before he handed the clothes over to me, he insisted I have sex with him. I said no; I wouldn't do it. He got upset, but he gave me the clothes because I was going to a church convention.

Later on, he kept pushing and pushing and showering me with gifts. He would purchase cards, put lots of money in them, and slide them through the mailbox. The only thing he didn't try to woo me with is jewelry, but he was constantly sending me flowers and feeding me and my two children, showering me with gifts over and over until I eventually gave in and became his secret lover.

I'm not proud of it, but in retrospect, the reason I gave in was because of greed. The low self-esteem I put myself through wasn't worth it. It got to a point where every time I saw him, I cringed. I literally cringed. I felt like I was going to throw up every time I saw him because I felt like I was selling my soul, and in actuality, I was. One day, when he took me to a BMW dealership in Emeryville, that broke the camel's back. I was with him and another older gentleman. They were both old enough to be my father, he asked me if I wanted a new car. I suppose that was meant to make me gush over him because it was a top-of-the-line vehicle back then, but I just said "OK."

When we got back to his office, what did he want in return? Sex. As long as I would continue to have sex with him, he was willing to buy me whatever I wanted. But I couldn't do it anymore. I refused the BMW and kept it moving. It lasted no more than a year, and that's how it stopped. I knew that if I accepted that BMW, I would have definitely been obligated, and I couldn't allow myself to do it. He challenged me with intimacy. Either you do what I ask or it all goes away because with money there's control, and he wanted complete control. I just couldn't be a kept woman anymore. I couldn't sell my soul like that. I didn't have any feelings for him, and honestly, over the course of the year, I could count the number of times we were intimate on one hand. He was old and really couldn't do anything anymore, but he challenged me and wanted control over me.

You can call me spoiled, selfish, and greedy. Because I had a job, I had money coming in, and I had my own car, but he offered me a better one for his own desire to dominate me. I not only allowed him to use me, I used myself. Because I felt degraded, my self-esteem was blown. I disrespected myself, and I disrespected other people. And because I felt guilty, I suffered. I wasn't able to see any real good in him and couldn't enjoy any of the time I spent with him. Although we didn't have anything in common, he was well groomed, well dressed, had all the money, wore lavish jewelry, and would come to pick me up in a white limousine sometimes. I just got caught up in greed, and after I lost both my parents, I felt uprooted and ungrounded.

Later, after it ended, I found out he was married. I was not aware of that at the time, and I was just devastated. And I said, "*How could I do that?*" That was just totally inappropriate, infidelity. It was just disgusting. I was just really devastated and upset. I had no right to do that, no right at all. I care about people and do not intentionally step on anyone's toes. I felt I was totally disrespectful to myself and other people. It's not a good feeling at all.

Being a secret lover meant allowing myself to be bought, myself to be bought. I sold my soul, and that was a terrible feeling. I've been there and done that, and I know I'm not the only one who has done it, and I think it's important to have integrity and have some integrity about yourself, and not to compromise your self-worth or accept less as a woman or a man because you feel desperate, or lonely, or you're getting up there in age and feel the need to have somebody and just accept whatever comes your way. It shouldn't be like that. You should wait on God. You live and learn, and sometimes, you go through adversity because of your choices, and you're gonna pay for it. If you sow a bad seed, a bad seed will bloom. If you sow a good seed, a good seed will come back. Now, I'm blessed. That's because I'm sowing a good seed. I am saved by grace, and I judge no one. But God forbid, I would never do that again.

My parents' house went through probate for a year, and then it was sold. The money was split three ways, a third for me and each of my siblings. So, I packed up my kids, and we moved to

San Leandro. After we moved to San Leandro, a girlfriend of mine introduced me to Tony, and we started dating. He spoiled me rotten and made provisions for my kids. He was one of the best men I ever dated. He loved my children, and I became very close with his mother, and his entire family were nice people. Tony was very loyal and had a lot of compassion, and to this day, he claims my kids as his two kids. He made sure all the bills were covered, that there was food on the table, and he even bought me a Mercedes. This time, I accepted, but when we broke up, I returned it. We're still very good friends, but we broke up because he had a problem with alcohol. He asked me to get back with him, but I didn't want to move backward; I wanted to move forward. However, I made a lifelong friend, and I have nothing but 100 percent respect for him.

After my relationship with Tony, I moved to Solano County. It was around this time I met my mentor, Jimmy Williams. She is like another mother to me and became my adoptive godmother. Without her, I wouldn't have had anybody to talk to. My son was in elementary school when I met her. She used to be his bus driver, and my son wanted us to meet. We met, and we just connected. And she became my backbone. This is what I mean when I say wait on God. I needed love and support in my life, and God made sure it made its way to me. When I stopped sowing bad seeds and started sowing good seeds, good came from them, and I to this day have two enduring friendships.

7

HOLLYWOOD AND COMPANY

Jesus bent down and started to write on the ground
with his finger. When He straightened up, He said to
them, "if any one of you is without sin, let him cast the
first stone at him or her."

John 8:6–7

While I began living in Solano County, I was still modeling
and working as a medical consultant. I started singing in a band
called Hollywood and Company. Hollywood was actually Robert
Jenkins. He was the lead singer, and we fell in love and got
married. We had a beautiful marriage. It was magnificent, and
I really enjoyed singing with the group. There's really not a bad
thing I can say about him. However, sadly, he had a gambling
addiction, and he chose gambling over me. Due to this, we
decided to part ways, and I filed for divorce.

It was an amicable split, and when we decided to part ways, he
moved out. He didn't have any money because he had gambled it
all away. I literally had to give him money to put his clothes and

accessories in storage because he didn't have the money to put a down payment on a storage unit. I also gave him money to move. We were together for about 10 years, and we split in 2011. I do not judge him. Even though I went through some financial strain due to his addiction, I know that addiction is an illness. I really don't believe it's something that people choose. Like having an addiction to drugs and alcohol, it's a disease, and I refuse to judge these people.

After we split, I stayed alone. After two marriages, relationships in between, and raising my children who were now adults, I felt it was time for me to spend time with myself and learn who I was. I had lost myself somewhere, and I decided to isolate myself and stay celibate. I didn't want to date anybody because I had been in unhealthy relationships, and I felt that because of past experiences, all I had to dish out was unhealthy. It was time to focus on me, and it was time for me to get me together. I stayed in isolation for seven years.

You might forget the pose but not the attitude.

LINDA JACKSON
Vocalist, Model & Fashion Consultant

Leave your mark, where ever you go.

Sexy is not about the body, but a woman with confidence.

8

HEARING GOD IN SILENCE

Let love and faithfulness never leave you. Bind them
around your neck, write them down on your tablet of
your heart. Then you will win the favor of God and man.
Trust in the Lord with all your heart and lean not to thy
own understanding; in all thy ways acknowledge him
and He will direct your path.

Proverbs 3:3–6

Although I decided to isolate myself, I was still going to church.
I had been a member of Mount Calvary Baptist Church for at
least a year, and we had a wonderful minister, Pastor Clayburn
Lea. I've made lasting friendships at Mount Calvary. One day, we
all decided to take a bus to LA to *The Price Is Right*.

I was called to be a contestant, and I can say I am a *Price
is Right* winner. I won a fire pit, gym equipment, a sauna, and
an indoor and outdoor TV. I didn't make it to the showcase
showdown, but I think I still racked up. If your prizes are not
delivered after 90 days, they pay you the amount of the prize in

cash. So, the only prize delivered was the gym equipment, the rest was paid to me in cash. I had a marvelous time, that was a start of a new beginning for me. I knew I had made the right decision and was headed in the right direction. I was enjoying life, looking at things differently, loving people, and loving myself.

When I won on The *Price is Right*, I knew my life was about to change for the better. I call it good energy. I repented, and I'd always been saved, I did all that I could to help others. It's called the gift of helps and charity. Before I knew it was the gift of helps, I found myself having a rescue ranger calling. I thought it was because of the way that I dressed and carried myself. I was always OK financially, so once again I found myself giving, I had to patiently wait on my blessing. It wasn't handed to me overnight. I had to wait on God.

I worked hard for my earthly material blessings. I went to work every day, I brought home a paycheck, I provided for my kids, I paid cash for all my furniture, and I rarely used my credit cards. Just about everything I owned I paid cash for because I was able to. Again I found myself taking care of others. Even when it came down to choosing a man at the time, I was a little naive. It seemed like they weren't self-sufficient enough. I'm not trying to stereotype, but it was like I'm not your mama; you must be self-sufficient and provide for yourself. And it just seemed like I ran into the same type of men back then. It was awful. When I decided to self-isolate, I was pretty content. I spent a lot of quality time with my oldest granddaughter Aiyanna Renee, my son's first born, she followed me everywhere. Now she's all grown up and has become CEO of Bazarb Media modeling agency.

From time to time I would get dolled up and go out with my girlfriends. Men would hit on me and ask me out, but I just said no. At that point in time, I needed to do me. When I decided to open up, I was truly disappointed, again he was not self-sufficient. I'm like Lord, what's going on? I found that men who are not self-sufficient tend to be clingy. It may not be their fault. It's just a lack of training. Well, I backed out of it because I did not want to draw the same type of individual, I refuse to engage in the same type of spiritual being. I've moved forward without turning back. We all have choices, let's start making the right ones. Love yourself so you can love others. Demand respect for yourself, and show some Integrity as a male or female. It's not just one-sided. God created Male and Female. God opened up my eyes. God helped me get through Isolation, seriously that wasn't easy. It gets lonely. Be careful what you ask for. I learned from various bruises. God had me look at myself in the mirror. HE taught me how to be patient with myself. I had to let go and let God have his way.

Let me share a little something with you. Rejection can be heart-wrenching leaving you psychologically and physically drained. causing you to never trust or love someone again. I'm sure we all have been there. Well, I can't thank God enough for the rejection. Handpick me oh Lord. My value did not come from people or accomplishments, it came from my creator. Staying focused and taking care of Linda has become a priority in my life.

Leaving all baggage behind. Moving forward, never looking back no matter how hard it may be.

Let's talk about having mental and physical strength, staying healthy in the mind, including the power of our tongue. Proverbs 18:21 Death and Life are in the power of the tongue those who talk will reap consequences. And those who love will eat of its fruits. We are what we speak. Do not allow people to control you. Husbands, Wives, Girlfriends, Boyfriends. Let's build one another up. Please do not tear or demolish their character.

Again we must learn how to be patient with ourselves. We must not accept less because we feel alone or invisible. Of course, none of us were created to live in isolation. Genesis 2:21-22 God recognized this and caused Adam to fall into a deep sleep. He then took one of Adam's ribs from him, which he fashioned into a woman, who was called Eve. Just because a person has money doesn't mean he or she is good for you. Make sure you look at his or her heart. Actions speak louder than words. Jesus said it's what's inside us that comes out. Our behavior flows from our hearts and out of our mouths. We all have power and control over our choices. Remember bad seed in, bad seed out. Good seeds will produce strong positive growth.

I would like to thank God for the time I spent alone. I learned to be careful who to trust. We should never share our personal history with everybody. Trust me it will backfire. People whom you think you can trust and share your burdens with are the ones who backstab you. They grin and laugh at you as soon as you walk away. Well, that's all I need to say.

Let me share another story with you. I tried to help an individual. It backfired during the time I spent alone. I tried to open up for a second time. But I still wasn't ready. I came to find out this individual has a lot of baggage, and I was like, not again I can't do this. There was too much baggage. Therefore, the first thing to mind was to let go and let God. I just let go. No judgment, we all must learn to move forward. But mental abuse is nothing to play with.

I would like to share that I haven't always been a saint. I'm not perfect, I'm only human. I had to learn how to forgive myself and forgive those who hurt me as well. I must bow and give all glory and honor to my Heavenly Father for his love, grace, mercy, patience, forgiveness, and salvation. Without him we are nothing. I'm grateful now just for life. I'm grateful to be able to open my eyes every day. I'm grateful for my job. I'm grateful to not be afraid to love again. I'm grateful that I can be respectful. When I decided to isolate myself I was pretty content. I spent a lot of my quality time with my oldest granddaughter Aiyanna, my son's first child. and I went to visit my brother frequently in prison.

Keep talking to God. He may seem silent, but that doesn't mean we should doubt Him. Its an invitation to press forward.

Linda Jackson (Yeh) Price is Right winner!

9
SAYING GOODBYE

I have set a rainbow in the clouds, and it will be
a sign of the covenant between me and the earth.
Genesis 9:13

My brother Victor passed away on March 23rd, 2021, from liver cancer. He was in prison all those years, and during that time, he got saved. I love him so much, and I appreciate him so much. He never got a shot at life. He never got a chance to go visit a park again, and he never got a chance to come to have dinner and enjoy Christmas. Could you imagine? A child: I was 21, he was 24 years old, and he never saw another day of freedom. He died at the age of 66 because the country is so racist. They wouldn't let him out. I went to the board countless times. My brother even had a mental breakdown, and then he came back and he was fine, and I was down for him. I went to Vacaville Prison and sat behind a wall and talked to him until I had to leave, just so I could show support. I was the one that visited him consistently. My sister, my nephew, and my daughter visited but not often. When he was in the hospice, my sister and my nephew visited him, but it was very difficult for him. He died in the hospice, but I was there every day from the time he was in the hospice until the day he crossed over and transitioned.

When my brother was sent to prison, my family was still grieving the loss of my mother, and my brother started using heroin. He wrote a couple of letters from prison asking us to forgive him when we were growing up. When I was working, he stole some of my coats that were in the closet and some of my clothes. I asked him who stole the clothes, and he denied it because he was on drugs and said that he didn't do it, but he actually did.

I feel he stayed in prison because of racism. He said, "I didn't deserve this. Why did they put me away like this?" All those years, my brother went through adversity. He was in the hole. He had a mental breakdown, but he survived it. After my father died, my sister and I took over, and we always sent him packages and money. I'd been sending money to a prison since 1980, and I just stopped in March of 2021. I went to a prison visiting my brother for years and years and years, and it was just a pleasure and a joy. We sat down and ate popcorn and talked about art, my family, and just had love for one another. It was just a blessing to be able to communicate and share quality time with him.

He passed away in Vacaville Prison, and I was there. I held his hand as he took his last breath. His blood pressure was very low, so his eyes were closed, but when he passed, he opened his eyes, and he told me "I love you. Thank you so much." And he kissed me. He held my hand real tight, and he transitioned. And I saw him taking his last breath as I was holding his hand. When the Lord was taking him up, it was like there was a roaring, like a volcano, a strong vibration, and my hand was just shaking when his body lifted up. His soul lifted up, and the Lord just took him. When I looked up, it was like I could see the glory. From that day, I had a different perspective on life. Because you're brought here, and we have a day to die, and God is real, I witnessed it for myself.

I know when a person dies it seems like people should be sad, but my brother was so tired because he had been there for over 45 years. And he said he was gonna be free, "I'm finally gonna be free. I don't have to live like this anymore." He told me he wanted to be cremated and to spread his ashes across the ocean because he wanted to be free. "I've been locked up for many years, and I want you to let me go." If he had not made this request we would have kept his ashes.

We had a service for my brother. I wrote his obituary, and I put some of my brother's artwork in it. He created a cartoon character called Vogee Ogee. It's so cute. It kind of looks like a clown and an egg. And everybody asked, "Who did this? You could make money from this," but I didn't have time. I think it could be a children's book or a cartoon, or a T-shirt. It's just something that he left that my sister and I have.

The beautiful thing is, before he passed, he had nothing but respect from the guards, the prisoners, the counselors, and even the warden. They wrote nothing but beautiful comments in his obituary: How he was a model inmate and how he tried to help everybody, and he loved everybody. He didn't get a chance in life, and I had to endure that.

The prison took his ashes, and they wouldn't allow us to be there on the boat when they spread them over the ocean. They called us and let us know when they were leaving. They took his urn to the middle of the ocean and spread them over Marin County. But they would not allow us to attend. That's the only thing that I regret, but this is what he wanted. If we had buried him, he would have gone in our family plot.

When he crossed over to be with the Lord, it was absolutely beautiful. I was able to see the power of the Lord just take over, and it was eye-opening. My perspective on life really changed on March 23rd, 2021.

My Brother Victor and daughter Demetra. Until we meet again. We will never forget you.

To Victor from your sister's Donna & Linda

In Our Heart

We thought of you today.
But that is nothing new.
We thought about you yesterday.
And days before that too.
We think of you in silence.
We often speak your name.
Now all we have are memories.
And your picture in a frame.
Your memory is our keepsake.
With which we will never part.
God has you in his keeping.
We have you in my heart.

Victor you will always be remembered and never forgotten.

Victor, your gift was precious.

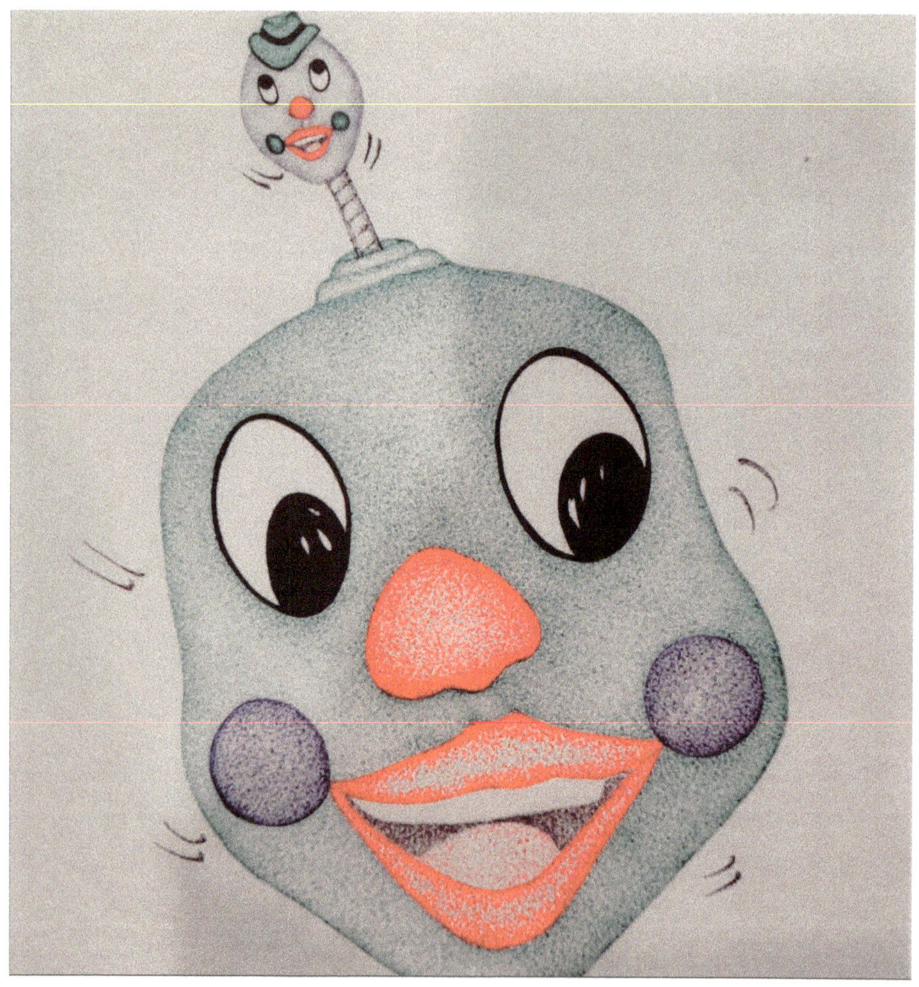

Victor had God-gifted hands.

10

SAYING GOODBYE

Ask and it will be given unto you. Seek and you will find;
and to him who knocks; the door shall be opened.
Matthew 7:7–8

Dear God, you have a special plan for your people. Help us to trust you to guide us where you want us to go. I am choosing to place my trust in you, my Redeemer. I know our eternal home is with you, but while we are here on earth, please lead us. Give us discernment to see which path to take and how to serve you. Help us to depend on your strength to go, where to go, where we've been called. Thank you for your unfailing love. And thank you for your love and mercy. In Jesus' name, amen.

Do not be afraid of who or what God has created in you. Love your creator, the almighty, omnipotent, undefeated God. Let's build self-esteem, physical and psychological empathy for others, and mental strength. Everything has a seed. If you plant trouble, trouble will return. God's seed is good. God has mended my broken past. The Lord is close to a broken heart, and He saved those who questioned their spirit. Even though we feel defeated, God is closer to us than we realize. He's always with us. We just have to believe and walk in faith. Walk in faith and not by sight.

There are signs and evidence when God is talking to you, speaking to your heart. I always say, "Let go, let God." You can tell when a person is not in sync with you. And you should not be with that person because of the signs. It's amazing how we tend to ignore the signs. A sign to look out for is no covenant. When I say covenant, I mean there's no promise, no covenant between the two. Another sign is when you meet somebody, and your significant other has no plans to marry. Another sign is if you ask the person if they're loyal and that person says no. Another red flag is they tend to draw you from your family; they don't want you to spend quality time with your family. It's all about him or her. It's me, me, me. Not sharing yourself with friends and family, isolating yourself just to that individual, that's when you know that that person is very needy. You become distant from loved ones.

Another sign is getting distracted from your goals. To prevent that, you have to be quiet and let God intercede. And sometimes in order to let God intercede when you've been through adversity, you have to go through isolation. In isolation, you can be very lonely, but you need that quality time for yourself and God so you can learn who you are as a person, and I'm going to tell you it's a trial. It's definitely a trial because you don't want to be in your house by yourself; you want to be around friends and family. I'm not saying you can't be around family and friends, but you're going to isolate yourself from companionship.

Everybody loves companionship. And when you don't have companionship, during the holidays—Valentine's, Thanksgiving, Christmas, New Year's—it's hard. I've been through that by myself. I just dealt with it. Was it lonely? Yes, but I dealt with it, and I'm a better person today. I have love for people. I'm not judging people. I remember growing up, I wasn't always humble. I had to come down off my high horse. Even though I had beautiful clothes, and I attracted people, it didn't matter. You can be beautiful, but you can be ugly inside. And that's something I hate to see. One thing I hate is a bitch, constantly badgering, running off at the mouth but saying nothing. It goes for both males and females. Have I been in that position before? Yes, but God has taken me to another level where I have been able to grow and share my innermost thoughts.

Another thing you don't want to play with is a broken heart. Don't intentionally try to break people's hearts because it's not good. It's not fair. Don't use that person. If you're coming out of a relationship, take some time and isolate yourself. If it's 30 days, 40 days, or 60 days, isolate yourself. Find yourself. Then, if you feel that you're ready, then you go ahead and talk to somebody else if you choose to. If you want to be a part of somebody's life, you can, but you've got to make sure there's no baggage because all you're doing is taking one problem into another problem. It's just problem after problem after problem.

I feel it's very inappropriate for people to ask about your past. I cannot stand it when you're in a new relationship and the other person asks you about your prior relationships. Why do you need to know about what happened yesterday? Why do you need to know about experiences from the past? Let's move on from the past. It's about today. Today is another day. I don't care what happened yesterday or what happened years ago. We have to live, learn, and grow from it. When we go through adversity, even though we cannot see it, it's God asking us to grow. Because of my suffering, I learned to have respect for people. We can't be greedy in relationships. Our blessings must come from God. Give from the heart, and don't accept less when your kindness is returned.

After my parents passed away, I had to be an adult. Even though I was an adult, I still had a child's mentality. I didn't have a mentor, and when you're young and naïve, you do stupid things. I feel that I lost a lot. I was out there by myself, trying to teach myself things. I feel there were a lot of things I lacked knowledge of. And I was easy to manipulate. "I'll give you this if you do this for me. I'll give you that if you do this for me." That's nothing but Satan. "If you make love to me, you can have whatever you want." Well, it's not just about the material; it's about integrity as a woman. Love yourself. Your jury box is your jury box. Do not allow anybody to control that. You control yourself and yourself only. God loves me. He forgives me, and I don't have anything to hide. You guys want to know who I am and who I was? That's who I was, but the person I am now? You can't touch me because I'm a woman of God. I'm going to always walk in faith, persevere, stay focused, and prosper.

We as women and we as men need to learn how to love ourselves, so we can love other people. If you can't love yourself, you can't love the other person. I'm sitting over here happy and content, and you're sitting over here miserable because you have that negative energy going on. I cannot get with the negative energy.

To be honest, I'm just now opening up and allowing people in my space. I've always had long-term relationships, and I'm waiting on God to send me the right person and not just jump into anybody's arms and sell myself short. We should not accept that, and I'm not gonna do that again. Yeah. I refuse to live that kind of life. So right now, it's amazing. It doesn't matter where I go. People see me in public on Facebook and always tend to ask me, "Why are you single? What are you doing?" Or "What have you done?" And they tend to ask me a lot of questions. "You're so beautiful. So, what are you doing? What happened?" Uh, it's just my choice.

In relationships, as soon as things go bad, all of a sudden, you become a booty call or other negative things. It's not fair to women, and it's not fair to men, either. There are some good men out there. You just have to show respect and know if it doesn't work out, it's not gonna work out. Let's just show each other respect and move on. We can be happy. Let's be friends and move on. That's how I work in life.

God has a special plan for everybody. Everybody has an assignment on earth. When I say I'm choosing to place my trust in you, we all have to choose and place our trust in Jesus Christ. I've been through adversity. I know what it's like to be up and down, but we all have a choice: Either you're going to live for

Christ, or you're going to die for Him. I choose to live for Him because I love Him unconditionally. I just want to be there as a sister to help other people, not just people outside, but in my household. Because first, before you can help others, where does it start? From home. My kids are not perfect. My kids go through adversity. My kids have problems. And my kids fight. However, because I'm a praying mother, I try to be patient. I try to prevent myself from yelling. I try to set an example as a mother and a grandmother. Does it work for me all the time? No. Because sometimes, even though you can be a mentor for somebody else, your children don't always listen to you. You're not going to get your kids to always listen to you. However, I love my children and grandchildren unconditionally.

Learning who I am as a person and my integrity as a woman was important. But the most important thing is my inner soul, loving who I am and who God created and forgiving myself. I had to forgive myself, and I asked God for forgiveness for the sins that I committed yesterday because God forgives us. God is a God of grace and mercy, and I had to learn to forgive myself and love myself.

Our eternal home is with Jesus Christ. Down here, we're just passing through. Up there, that's our eternal home, and either you're going to believe it or not. There is a heaven, and there is a hell, and that's someplace I do not want to go. I don't even want to visit. I don't want to even entertain it. I believe there is another dimension and getting over to the other side and seeing all my family. I would love to see my brother, my mom, my dad, my aunt, my grandmother. All of my family is gone except myself, my sister, and my aunt, but as far as my immediate family, it's just my sister and me.

Give us discernment to see which path to take and how to serve you. Do I have a discerning spirit? Yes, I do. Discernment means give us guidance, Lord. Allow me to be able to see. Allow me to be able to help. I can only do so much, but wherever God leads me and guides me, that's where I'm going. Give me the discernment to be able to help others, and give me the discernment to be able to make good choices. Give me discernment to be able to love and not judge. Help us to depend on your strength. We all need God's strength because when we are down, we have to depend on him. He walks in front of us, in the back of us, he walks beside us, and he walks on the other side. So, he's holding us up all the time, like Paul, when Jesus told him to walk on water.

Thank you, Lord, for your love, your grace, your mercy, your endurance, your patience, and unconditional love. In Jesus' name, amen.

Remember you never really lose until you stop trying. Be patient with yourself.

Story Terrace

www.ingramcontent.com/pod-product-compliance
Lightning Source LLC
Chambersburg PA
CBHW040126150726
48005CB00015B/2381